False Start

The Peters and the Prodigals of the Faith

Dr. Nedna-Ann Johnson

ISBN: 979-8-9944157-2-6

Library of Congress Cataloging-in-Publication Data
Nedna-Ann Johnson
False Start
Take hold of redemption. Complete the Kingdom assignment

Published by: K SCRIBES CONSULTING & PUBLISHING
Metuchen, New Jersey, USA
kscribesinfo@gmail.com

Our books may be purchased in bulk for promotional, educational, training or business use. For inquiries, please contact the publisher via email:kscribesinfo@gmail.com

Edited and designed by Chapter 10 (chaptr10publish@gmail.com)

Printed in the United States of America

All Scriptures are quoted from the New King James translation of the Bible unless otherwise noted.

Dedication

To the Peters and prodigals of the Faith, those who once stewarded intimacy with the Lord but stumbled; who made missteps, neglected their altars and assignments, or issued quiet or public denials and betrayals, yet have since wept bitterly in the shadows.

It is time to arise, says the Lord: *"Go tell my disciples and PETER..."* He has called you by name, pulling you from seats of distraction and instability in which you have sat far too long, and from pits of pity and condemnation.

"We have work to do." Arise and build.

Contents

Dedication *v*

Acknowledgement *vii*

Note to Readers *viii*

CHAPTER 1. Can I Make a Comeback? 1

CHAPTER 2. I Am an Athlete? 7

CHAPTER 3. Benefits of the Kingdom Race 17

CHAPTER 4. The Graveyard of Condemnation 23

CHAPTER 5. The Prodigals Are Coming Home 29

Acknowledgement

To my Elder, the late Dr. Monique Cunningham. I do not believe the Lord could have chosen a better person to stand in the gap for me during that season of my journey. Thank you for taking me under your wings when I was most vulnerable, and for encouraging me, even in our final moments together, to remain with the Lord.

I honor you always in my memory, my thoughts, and my steps. You are now in heaven, and I imagine you among the great cloud of witnesses, dancing in celebration that this work has finally been published. Your voice "Girl, get it together" carried me through. I got it together, my Elder. I am still in the race. I am making my way .

To the Holy Ghost, my endearing companion and constant company, my ally and advocate. You taught me the power and peace of being alone but not lonely. I am never alone, because You are always present. Thank You for being faithful.

Note to Readers

One truth I have gleaned from my years of intentionally pursuing Christ is this: if the flow stops, or the well appears to dry up, it is never because there is fault in Christ, nor because He did not rise and is not alive. I know that He did, and that He is, because He has left upon me too many imprints to ever be denied.

If the flow stops, or the well dries, it is I. I am out of alignment with the government of His great Kingdom. Somewhere, somehow, I stumbled; I lost my footing. And so, to honor the truth of who He is, and to refuse the kingdom of darkness its relentless attempt to amass evidence against what is already undisputed, I must arise, gird my loins, and contend.

For it is not His truth that I contend to uphold; that truth can never be shaken. It is my own crown and my place on the right side of heaven's history that I am contending for.

It has already been written. The war has already been

won. My place is secured, based on whose side I choose to fight on. I choose Heaven. And so, I contend.

Will you arise? Or will you stay down and wallow? Will you, through passivity, allow yourself to be drafted as a reserve in Satan's army, fighting a war he has long since lost? Choice is man's most important power. Think.

I plant my stake with Heaven. I lay hold of the Kingdom's reward. I set my face like flint, that no man, and no demon in hell, will take my crown.

CHRIST IS KING.

Chapter ONE

Can I Make a Comeback?

Go tell His disciples and Peter (Mark 16:7)

It was about 8:45 a.m. I do not remember the exact day, but I was on Route 1, driving to Cranberry for work. Determined to avoid arriving late, I was traveling at close to 80 miles per hour, a pace we Jamaicans would term "*bird speed.*" I chuckled to myself as I watched the newer-model vehicles sped past me on both sides at roughly 30–35 miles per hour. Then a soft whisper stirred within my spirit and echoed in my ears: *false start.* An undeniable knowing settled upon me. This was the Holy Spirit, not only naming the title, but revealing the very pillar of the next book I was to write.

It had been a few years since I sat down with true focus

and intentionality to produce a written work on behalf of the Kingdom. Why? Events leading up to that moment had left me carrying more than bottled-up emotion. I had missed it with God through disobedience and selfishness, and found myself struggling, through repeated attempts, to return to that place in Him and with Him before I felt worthy enough to put my hands to the Kingdom's business.

I had withdrawn and reduced my life to day-by day routines: processing, grieving, replaying the cycle of events again and again, as though some miracle might transport me back in time to make decisions with hindsight and swap outcomes. *Will I ever make it back to the Place?* was a question I asked often.

Yet one thing never died, nor did it seem willing to die. There remained within me a persistent desire not merely to be saved and live an average life, but to be a believer who leaves a mark on heaven's history.

I also knew the sacrifice it had taken to reach the place from which I had stumbled.. Now, looking up from where I stood, the mountain appeared insurmountable. Voices of condemnation rang continually in my ears, and for months I wrestled in that space, angry at both the person directly connected to my fall and myself.

I wrestled double mindedness, instability and unforgiveness. I wrestled between returning to rekindle the flames of my prayer altar and yielding to a lie, attempting to salvage the very thing that had been intentionally sent to throw me off course.

In all this, I had become numb on the inside, yet I fought to keep my heart from hardening. I remembered a tool the Holy Spirit had taught me years earlier. It felt as though I was being made to retake the lesson, but I embraced humility and chose obedience, praying for the person involved while asking God for mercy and strength to steady the reins of my heart.

The Lord, my Father, was merciful and patient, correcting me even as He built me up. "False start," Holy Spirit? I asked. He did not respond, because He knew I heard and understood the instruction. This was His way of inviting me to journey with Him on an assignment that would not only draw me fully out of my present rut, but also allow me to scribe a trail so that others might know there is always a way of escape, though the outcome is directly connected to choice.

I got home and delved into study of the ancient Sword—the Scriptures—to research. My mind was buzzing: excited, overthinking, dramatic. *I must chronicle a pathway for those beside me and those coming up behind me, while reclaiming my own redemption.* "Holy Spirit, You know me so well," I chuckled. My dramatic flair is always heightened when I am called to write.

So I drew my sword (bible), and pen the scepter of authority I know He has gifted me, and whispered softly, in my inner voice, "Great One, let us journey."

Then silence filled the atmosphere, lingering for days. This was His way of signaling: *Calm down, Nedna.* I took a deep breath and repeated it to myself. *Calm down, Nedna.* Then I asked the question that would not let me go: How do I write about something I have not yet fully overcome? I am still wrestling, Holy Ghost.

Days later, He sent His response—simple, firm, and unmistakable: *"Get over it. Fresh Start. Phil 3:10-16. All that happened was within the boundaries of My will. A season of restoration is on the horizon. Do not miss the window. Focus, so that you may step into it with Joy and gladness. You must leave the past behind intentionally, even if it requires straining and pressing to do so. This must be done so that you may lay hold of the very thing, or things, for which I laid hold of you. Joel 2:25"*

This was a word of compassion, not one of chastisement or rebuke. Such words usher us into a deeper level of relationship with our God. "*Get over it*" so that you may make room for what is coming. The process of forgetting is necessary to make room for the things which are worth remembering: payback, recompense, and double for the years lost as a result of "that which I sent among you."

There are times and seasons in the believer's life, seen in the stories of Joseph, Job, Moses, and David, when "that which I sent among you" shows up. Yet even then, it unfolds within the boundaries of His will.

Nothing is done outside the purpose and boundaries of His will. The mature will grasp this. Those boundaries are established by His will and His purpose. Job was tested within the boundaries of His will. Joseph's betrayal by his brothers unfolded within the boundaries of His will and within the scope of His purpose. David, though anointed king, chosen and set apart, was permitted to wander the wilderness in hiding, living beneath the fullness of his calling and anointing, yet still within the boundaries of God's will and purpose. In the same way, He allows us to go through our own seasonal measures, some lasting months, others years, but always within the boundaries of His will and purpose. He sends and allows things *within* those boundaries.

Can you be comforted by this? I can.

I chose to be comforted by whatever the Lord has chosen to allow, do, or touch in my life, knowing it is within the boundaries of His will and purpose. My prayer is that this truth will also comfort you. What you experienced and endured was not for nothing, but for His greater purpose, and within the boundaries of His will.

I pray that this what currently challenges you will bring you into deeper level of perspective. We all pass through seasons where we want to give the cup back. Even Christ faced such a moment: "Lord if it is possible, let this cup pass from me." (Matt 26:39). God in heaven! That was a hard place to be. Yet what feels hard is measured at different levels and intensity for all of us, according to what we are assigned to carry.

I received the word with humility and gratitude from the mouthpiece through whom it was sent. It was timely, and I knew it was the word of the Lord, spoken sternly, as I had experienced Him do a few times when I hesitated to move on an instruction.

I crawled into my place of prayer, uttering what felt like the bare minimum. Yet sometimes the simplest prayers carry the greatest weight: "Jesus, Jesus, Jesus, please help your daughter." I cannot tell you how many times that was all I had. And still, the Father spoke.

Chapter

TWO

I Am an Athlete?

My mind was transported back to my high school days and of course an activity that I was not so fond of—Physical Education, or P.E.

Unfortunately, the class was mandatory, leaving me with no choice but to suit up and attempt tryouts in search of a tribe within the arena of sports. I would much rather have sat quietly under a tree, absorbed in my English literature book, but I remember having no such luck.

I just knew it in my gut, even before I was mature enough to understand what a *Knowing* was, I was already experiencing them. Long before I stepped onto the field, I knew I was neither cut out for nor called to sports. A spectator? Absolutely! An active participant on the field? No!

Reluctantly, I shuffled forward in line to prove my knowing to the coach.

Fist trail and first attempt: the 100 meter dash. "Marks. Set Go" I launched forward with all the speed that I had been blessed with. Just imagine me bursting through the finish line—*dead last.* That was the term used in Jamaica for the slowest of the slow, those who lost races at every level. I was not shaken though. I already knew this was not my space.

"Perhaps there would be better luck in trying the hurdles?" said the coach,

"I highly doubt it." I replied. "If I cannot run fast in a straight line on a flat surface, it does not seem wise to attempt it while jumping over elevated objects. I think this is common sense Coach."

Coach responded, "Nothing beats a trial but a failure!" A sudden gust of motivation rose from his words, just enough to carry me toward the first hurdle. I ran, postured to jump, and then calculated mid-stride that this was a terrible idea. I did not finish the race. I happily conceded at the resistance of the very first hurdle. I did not care what anyone thought. After all, we cannot all be good at everything.

What about the relays? Perhaps that would work, leveraging the speed of teammates. Unfortunately, no matter which leg I was assigned, there was always someone faster, someone who seemed born for life on the track, waiting to contend with me. They each outran me to the finish. I was genuinely happy for those who had found their calling, while quietly knowing it was not mine.

Much like my distaste for calculus, and mathematics in general, unless the answer appeared quickly with the help of a calculator, I found myself asking aloud, hoping to gather like-minded comrades: "Why is this course mandatory if some of us already know we will not become mathematicians or athletes in the world at large?". Still, I hold dearly the memory of the one friend who stood with me through those challenging times.

I bounced about under the sun just enough to earn my passing grade for effort and attendance. While others made the school team and advanced to competitions against rival schools, some even progressing to junior trials, I remained a faithful supporter, firmly positioned as a spectator under the mango tree of the school yard, literature books in hand, Later, my support shifted to the bleachers at the national stadium. The love for track and field was infectious across the island. We followed and watched many who are now among the greatest in the world rise from humble beginnings to claim their medal and secure their place in the annals of sporting history.

My "maturity" in athletics came not on the track, but in the stands, moving from the bleachers to the grandstand once I began earning a living and could afford a better seat. *Lol.*

Yet here I am, years later, penning a book on false starts at the instruction of the Holy Ghost. I sit with Him for insight on how to transcribe His message, and He moves my spirit, thoughts and pen to follow the trail of an athlete.

I had heard it referenced often throughout my years of church attendance that the life of the believer is akin to one automatically enlisted into both a war and a race. Strikingly, however, it was always the words *war* and *warfare* that made me sit up with keen interest. And this is curious, because I am a peacemaker. I do not enjoy conflict. I prefer peace and despise discord. I am always striving to keep the balance.

But! Satan has tried me, and in the past I have been drawn out more times than I care to admit. If he were ever inclined to honesty, which I highly doubt, he would have admit that in every instance, I first chose forbearance and peace with those through whom he moved against me. It was only at the breaking point that conflict ensued, resulting in collateral damage that extended beyond the spiritual.

I have since matured, and continue to mature, in Jesus' Name. I now choose to pull myself up in remembrance of who my fight is with and where the battlefield lies.

As I reflect more deeply, my mind is telling me that I have not only read this truth in the Scriptures—"The race is not for the swift nor the battle for the strong…"—but I have also heard it preached repeatedly in sermons over the years. Did selective hearing play a role? Were those the times in the distant past when I may have fallen asleep in church? *I do not do that anymore, glory to God.*

So why did my mind choose to register *war* and *warfare* more readily than *athlete*? Perhaps that is a book for another time. Or perhaps it is a lesson I am now being invited to journey through.

I leaned back in my chair and took a moment to stretch, drawing in a deep breath. *I am an athlete?!* By virtue of accepting Christ, I had been drafted, not only into war, but into the very thing I thought I had successfully outrun all those years ago as a high schooler.

If you know the Holy Ghost, you know He has a sense of humor. He chuckled as the lightbulb came on in my mind. I kept my head down and my pen moving. He had me.

This was His umpteenth attempt to get me back *on track* after my false start. He has always pulled me out through either reading a book or writing one. This time, however, it was particularly challenging. My delay in responding to His instruction that "we have work to do" resulted in setbacks across lines I had already been fully delivered me from.

You must protect your deliverance. It is a deception to believe that if you treat deliverance lightly, everything will still turn out fine. No. One can fall back into former pits, and more often than not, the latter digs are harder to escape. Some, as depicted in Scripture, do not make it back at all.

Protect your deliverance. Cut off any hand, foot or person who disregards your boundaries or tries to convince you that you are doing too much, or that you are too radical.

I once believed I could not make it back, but thank God for His enduring love. The fact that I have written this book, and that you are now reading it, means that the same grace has been extended to you to enable your comeback. Don't waste it. Don't take it lightly. Don't abuse it.

In my doubt, the Holy Ghost kept challenging me to challenge Him. It is that call to persistence that He ensures becomes the first impression tugging on your heart each morning as you open your eyes. You simply know, *I need to get it together.* Like clockwork, the stirrings settles on your consciousness, reminding you that while it is understood that you are not perfect, it is also evident that you are not giving the fullest measure of yourself in your current state of imperfection.

To move toward perfection, you must make the deliberate choice to step out of limbo. Choice and obedience must align and move into activation.

I finally embraced His grace and yielded. He then began to walk me through the parallels, the pros and cons of the life of an athlete, specifically track and field. Not all athletes reach victory on their first attempt, and over time, the rules governing penalties for false starts have changed:

Historical Context of False Start Rules

- **2003-2009**: One false start was permitted for the entire field; any subsequent false start resulted in disqualification of the offending athlete.
- **Pre-2023**: One false start was allowed per athlete before disqualification.
- **Modern Rule (World Athletics/Olympics)**: One false start results in immediate disqualification for the offending athlete.

The rules have grown increasingly stringent over time in the games of the world system. Yet, even so, athletes who are disqualified are not barred forever. They are often granted the opportunity to return in the next cycle, and some come back to claim the gold.

Likewise, redemption remains possible for the believer as long as life still runs through the body. Only those who choose to stay down, who accept defeat, fail to cross the line. No one receives the crown without staying in the race.

The Believer's Rules

1. Competing Lawfully (2 Timothy 2:5)

An athlete does not receive the crown unless he competes according to the rules. In the same way, believers must abide by the principles of the Word to qualify for victory.

2. Running with Discipline (1 Corinthians 9:24-27)

This requires self-control in everything—focus, precision, and clarity of aim, with eternity as the mark. We do not shadowbox or run aimlessly, but instead exercise intense discipline, like trained athletes. This includes respecting the weight and value of time given to our stewardship, setting clear spiritual objectives, and making purposeful contributions to the agenda of the Kingdom with the gifts and tools in our possession. Time is a currency.

3. Upholding and Practicing the Principal Commandment (Matthew 22:37-39)

Love God and your neighbor. The believer's walk is governed by this fundamental principle which guides our actions, relationships, and faith journey in every area of life.

In the end, this race is not about flawless starts, but faithful finishes. False starts do not disqualify us from God's purpose; surrender does. As long as breath remains, grace remains, and the call to rise, realign, and run again still stands. The crown is not reserved for the swift or the strong, but for those who choose endurance, who submit to discipline, obey the rules of the Kingdom, and keep their eyes fixed on eternity. Stay in the race. Guard your deliverance. Run with intention. For the One who called you is faithful to see you through to the finish line.u is faithful to see you through to the finish line.

Chapter

THREE

Benefits of Staying in and Finishing the Kingdom Race

I paused to think—don't we all love to be associated with the winning team? A reccurring reminder during athletics championships back in school was "Don't be a *wagonist*," hopping on only after a team or athlete became popular. It was considered an honorable thing to choose your team and stand with them from start to finish, win, lose, or draw. To be associated with an honorable loss was far better than being a *wagonist.*

An imperishable crown and eternal life are promised on one condition: endurance. All who finish receive the crown of life, regardless of swiftness, speed, or strength. Finishers get their prize.

Were you entrusted by the Lord with a work to execute on His behalf, only for it to fall flat due to one missteps or another?

Did you take off like a tornado in zeal, forgetting to tarry with Him for His blueprint?

Did you claim His work as "my own," injecting ego and pride and taking His glory?

Did you deploy the hand of Uzzah due to impatience to "help" sustain God's work, only to discover that God will not share His glory, and so He withdrew Himself from your haste? (2 Samuel 6:6)

Did you neglect your secrete place, forgetting that Kingdom business cannot be flesh- or self-sustained?

Did you lose consecration and authority through disobedience, dishonor, sexual immorality?

Did you trade the heavenly vision for earthly approval and applause?

Has your heart since mourned daily for what you know you traded by making light of it?

Have you longed to return to the place of being a useful tool in the Master's hand, yet found yourself battling condemnation and thoughts of inadequacy at every attempt?

Have you resigned yourself to a norm you know is far below God's standard for you?

The Lord is calling you back to service and stewardship. If you will risk it all on Him one more time and say, "I will arise and go to my Father" (Luke 15:18). He will meet you at your point of limitation, make His strength perfect in your weakness, and restore your altar, fire, call, and commission.

He is declaring that the qualification bar is still set by Him—not by our righteousness, but by His. Your time has come to be plucked as a branch from the fire. The accuser standing nearby will find no legal ground to hinder this move. If, in humility of heart, you embrace repentance and turn, divine justice speaks on your behalf and in your favor (Zechariah 3:2).

He asked me to scribe and remind all who will hear and heed that He has always been known to call, anoint, qualify, and appoint from the ranks of the chiefest of sinners: the betrayer (Peter), the murderer (Moses), the adulterer (David), the bounty hunter (Paul), the runner (Jonah), and even a thief on the cross granted last-minute access into the Kingdom's inheritance. All because they were courageous enough to rise beyond yesterday's errors and earnestly lay hold of His divine way of escape.

The call to embrace salvation and Kingdom citizenship is the divine way of escape from the clutches of hell and the kingdom of darkness. This escape came at a cost: the precious blood of the firstborn Son, Christ Jesus. A true understanding of Christ's sacrifice ought to move us toward consecration and willing sacrifice on behalf of the Kingdom and its agenda. Authentic faith demands that we hold nothing above Christ, even when obedience makes us appear foolish in the eyes of men. To gain Christ, we must be prepared to relinquish what we love most in this life.

He asked me to write and remind the people, as I myself have been reminded, that the price has already been paid. He paid it in full, fully aware of all that you and I would have done. Our false starts were factored in, and yet grace still make room for us to arise and steward whatever assignment He entrusted into our hands.

With the fullness of His love, He is calling us not to remain down, wallowing in self-pity, trip-ups and missteps, but to rise and move forward with all our might. Run, walk, limp, crawl, or even roll if you must! Lean on a brother or sister. On tracks across the world stage, athletes have finished races in every imaginable posture, driven by a single resolve to cross the finish line. For some, the medal was no longer in grasp, but after the price they had paid training to get to the world stage, they decided giving up before crossing the finish line would be betrayal of purpose and a disservice to self.

Will you do a disservice to your soul by stopping short of the finish line? Then resolve, by grace, to finish the race.

He is the ultimate King of comebacks. Just as the kingdom of darkness calculated perfectly and still missed it with Jesus, so too does it miscalculate concerning us. As sons and daughters of the Kingdom of heaven, even our missteps are sealed by grace, causing us, if we contend, to arrive at the perfect score. We are backed by heaven, and we ourselves are sent forth as words carrying eternal weight. Once released into this realm, we cannot fall to the ground. We must accomplish the purpose for which we were sent (Jeremiah 1:12).

Chapter

FOUR

The Graveyard of Condemnation

(The Peter vs. Judas & Saul response)

One of my favorite preachers, whose name I will withhold to keep the peace, once said in a sermon: "If you ever had the anointing of God resting on you, you know it. And you also know when it lifts or has left you." Scripture confirms this repeatedly—1 Samuel 10: 6–9; 15:23; 16:14). Within these same passages, we also see the sobering consequences for repeated disobedience to God's commands and instructions.

Littered across Scripture, and even in the present day, we observe two contrasting responses among those who experienced false starts. One response is humility: retreating to the secret place in repentance, pursuing mercy, and allowing God to restore what was disrupted. The other response is pride: remaining puffed up in self and resorting to performance and theatrics to maintain visibility, relevance, and perceived authority. It is deeply disheartening to witness anyone choose the latter, the graveyard of condemnation.

Judas and Saul are examples of those who chose to camp in that graveyard. Peter, by contrast, responded to Jesus' summons. I too have decided to show up, so that the Lord may make for Himself a great name, as He sees fit, and receive His due glory.

Do not camp there! To do so is to call God wicked. Cowards opt to take the train. They get off one leg before the finish line, then stage a dramatic crossing to create the illusion that they ran faithfully from start to finish. I am not unfamiliar with dramatic flair myself, but shortcut maneuvers do not go unnoticed in the Kingdom where everything must be done honorably and in truth. You will not be awarded a crown only to be found out after some years in Heaven, with a chance to plead for mercy. No! You will simply be told: "I do not know you." Do not gamble with your salvation or your calling. Count the cost.

Having known Him, you also know that He is merciful. If He has ever pulled you out of anything, you are already acquainted with the mercy of God. That mercy is being extended now, but is not available for abuse. Grace is not a license to stay wallowing in sin; rather, it is the empowerment by which we are enabled to live according to Christ's standard, if we lean into it and chose not to abuse it.

Wake up! A book of remembrance is now opened unto you.

"Then those who feared the LORD spoke to one another, and the LORD listened and heard them; so a book of remembrance was written before Him for those who fear the LORD and who meditate on His name. 'They shall be Mine,' says the LORD of hosts, 'on the day that I make them My jewels. And I will spare them as a man spares his own son who serves him.' Then you shall again discern between the righteous and the wicked, between one who serves God and one who does not serve Him" (Malachi 3:16–18).

Embrace your great day in God.

"For behold, the day is coming, burning like an oven, and all the proud, yes, all who do wickedly will be stubble. And the day which is coming shall burn them up," Says the LORD of hosts, "That will leave them neither root nor branch. But to you who fear My name, the Sun of Righteousness shall arise with healing in His wings; And you shall go out and grow fat like stall-fed calves. You shall trample the wicked, for they shall be ashes under the soles of your feet on the day that I do this," says the LORD of hosts.

The graveyard of condemnation—the place of unresolved pride, rebellion, and false alignment—becomes fertile ground for the flourishing of the Jezebel and

Saul spirits. One seeks to extinguish the fire rising within God's true sons; the other hurls spears at the heads of the anointed. In the end, both spirits destroy their carriers." Judas met his end there, having accepted a bribe to carry out a wicked assignment. He fulfilled the role, but he was destroyed in the end.

What are spears, Lord? *They are smear campaigns, intimidation, religious shackles, gang ups, deception, temptations, doubt, and sinful thoughts.* These are weapons the believer must deflect with the shield of faith and prayer (Ephesians 6:16), rising out of the pit before destruction takes hold.

The Kingdom has tribes, but it is not a club or clique of elitists. We are sons and stewards serving one agenda and one King. This is not a competition for who shines the brightest or appears the most anointed. Rather, it is one Body—many parts, each unique, each intentionally crafted to contribute in unison—producing one harmonious declaration: **Christ is King**.

There is one Master Potter, the Holy Ghost, who leads us into all truth. As we are guided to lay hold of our unique identities, He molds us into a representation of excellence.

The Bible is already written, yet it is alive. You and I are walking out the portions we were written into. This is why it is a spiritual book, continually releasing fresh revelation to those who will make a demand on it in the Spirit. We worship the Father in spirit and in truth. We come to know Him by the Spirit. And according to the strength of our sacrifice, our portion of the "greater works" will be birthed in and through us, bringing glory to our Creator and King.

The Spirit of the Lord is groaning, urging us to dive deep and go high as spiritual explorers—pressing forward despite the mistakes and past false starts. He desires not only to reveal Himself to seekers, but to build us into beacons, bright luminaries, through whom He draws all men unto Himself.

Chapter

FIVE

The Prodigals Are Coming Home

It is difficult to recall a world-renowned athlete who does not publicly acknowledge and express gratitude for their coach. Arrival has a way of clarifying perspective. In hindsight, the tough love, persistent encouragement, relentless pressing, uncomfortable confrontations, and even closed-door disagreements are recognized for what they truly were—acts rooted in care, purpose, and a desire for excellence.

The Holy Ghost can be hard on us sometimes, much like guardians and helpers who genuinely mean us well. He often stirs us at the stillest hours of the night or day, when the temperature has dropped, the blanket is warm, and life's small comforts have settled gently around us. Just when we have decided to rest, slow down, or "do nothing for once," He disrupts our plans.

It is often in these moments that He draws near and

whispers, "Attend to this quickly," or "Get up and pray now," or "This is the season to do this thing." The immediate response is often resistance: *Tomorrow, Lord. Maybe later. I don't feel ready. There is still time.* We turn instead to what we believe is more urgent or more important, only to realize, sometimes when we are already deep underwater, the gravity of the error.

For many of us who went astray, our departure did not resemble the prodigal son leaving with bags of worldly riches, as depicted in the parable (Luke 15). Rather, we left carrying the substance of the Kingdom of our Father. We went with gifts bestowed by the Holy Spirit. We went with seeds of the Word planted in our young, fertile hearts.

Some of us set those gifts aside, counting them as insignificant. Others carried them into foreign systems, trading Kingdom substance for worldly validation while embracing the doctrines and patterns of the world system. As Scripture records: "And not many days after, the young son gathered all together and took his journey into a far country and their wasted his substance with riotous living" (Luke 15:13).

Yet truth cannot stay hidden forever. The heart of the Lord is declaring: "The hour is coming, and now is, when the true worshipers shall worship the Father in spirit and in truth: for the Father seeks such to worship Him" (John 4:23).

He is calling back the hearts of His prodigals! He is not seeking perfection, but sincerity. Not flawless resumes, but yielded hearts. Not those who never strayed, but those who will return, repent, and realign.

You are true sons, not bastards. You have been broken, yes, but broken for service. The scales have been removed from your eyes. He has allowed your options to be exhausted, not as punishment, but as mercy, so that no counterfeit satisfaction could be found in your way. As it is written, "And when he had spent all, there arose a mighty famine in that land and he began to be in want" (Luke 15:4). This is a spiritual want, a void only He can fill. Pick up the pearls you so foolishly cast before swine and head Godward.

The Word says he came to himself and said "I will arise and go to my father, and I will say unto him, father, I have sinned against heaven and before thee, And am no more worthy to be called thy son: make me as one of thy hired servants (Luke 15:18, 19)." In other words, he said, I have sinned against home. Nevertheless, I am returning to serve. I chose service! And what greater position exists in the Kingdom than that of serving in the Father's house?

Make haste and escape from Babylon! The Father is waiting. Run home. Run well.

To contact or follow Author Nedna-Ann Johnson:

kscribesinfo@gmail.com

@Nedna-Ann Johnson

@nednaannjohnson

@KingdomScribes

Other Books by Dr. Nedna-Ann Johnson

www.ingramcontent.com/pod-product-compliance
Lightning Source LLC
LaVergne TN
LVHW090618110826
845146LV00001B/447

* 9 7 9 8 9 9 4 4 1 5 7 2 6 *